Put Beginning Readers on the Right Track with
ALL ABOARD READING™

The All Aboard Reading series is especially designed for beginning readers. Written by noted authors and illustrated in full color, these are books that children really want to read—books to excite their imagination, expand their interests, make them laugh, and support their feelings. With fiction and nonfiction stories that are high interest and curriculum-related, All Aboard Reading books offer something for every young reader. And with four different reading levels, the All Aboard Reading series lets you choose which books are most appropriate for your children and their growing abilities.

Picture Readers
Picture Readers have super-simple texts, with many nouns appearing as rebus pictures. At the end of each book are 24 flash cards—on one side is a rebus picture; on the other side is the written-out word.

Station Stop 1
Station Stop 1 books are best for children who have just begun to read. Simple words and big type make these early reading experiences more comfortable. Picture clues help children to figure out the words on the page. Lots of repetition throughout the text helps children to predict the next word or phrase—an essential step in developing word recognition.

Station Stop 2
Station Stop 2 books are written specifically for children who are reading with help. Short sentences make it easier for early readers to understand what they are reading. Simple plots and simple dialogue help children with reading comprehension.

Station Stop 3
Station Stop 3 books are perfect for children who are reading alone. With longer text and harder words, these books appeal to children who have mastered basic reading skills. More complex stories captivate children who are ready for more challenging books.

In addition to All Aboard Reading books, look for All Aboard Math Readers™ (fiction stories that teach math concepts children are learning in school) and All Aboard Science Readers™ (nonfiction books that explore the most fascinating science topics in age-appropriate language).

All Aboard for happy reading!

To Sir Richard,
the feet beneath my knees—C.D.W.

To my family and friends—J.C.

Special thanks to Linda Honan, Education Director, Higgins Armory
Museum, Worcester, Massachusetts.

Text copyright © 1998 by Catherine Daly-Weir. Illustrations copyright © 1998 by Jeff Crosby.
All rights reserved. Published by Grosset & Dunlap, a division of Penguin Putnam Books for
Young Readers, 345 Hudson Street, New York, NY 10014. ALL ABOARD READING and
GROSSET & DUNLAP are trademarks of Penguin Putnam Inc. Published simultaneously in
Canada. Printed in the U.S.A.

Library of Congress Cataloging-in-Publication Data

Daly-Weir, Catherine.
    Knights / by Catherine Daly-Weir ; illustrated by Jeff Crosby.
      p. cm. — (All aboard reading. Level 2)
    Summary: Follows the life and training of a seven-year-old page in England in 1415 who
dreams of becoming a squire and hopes someday to be dubbed a knight.
      1. Knights and knighthood—Juvenile literature. [1. Knights and knighthood. 2. England—
Social life and customs—1066-1485. 3. Middle Ages.] I. Crosby, Jeff, ill. II. Title. III. Series.
CR4513.D35 1998
940.1'088'355—dc21   97-50347
                                                                                                          CIP
                                                                                                          AC

ISBN 0-448-41857-6   D E F G H I J

ALL ABOARD READING™

Station Stop
2

Knights

By Catherine Daly-Weir
Illustrated by Jeff Crosby

Grosset & Dunlap • New York

This is William.

William lives in England.

It is the year 1415.

And England is at war

with France.

William's father is a knight.

It is his job to help protect

the people of England.

Someday William hopes to be

a knight too.

Knights are soldiers who fight
on horseback.

They wear heavy suits of armor

to keep them safe in battle.

William is seven now.

He is old enough to be a page.

William says good-bye to his mother

and his sister.

He is leaving his family

and going to live

at Lord James's castle.

His father will take him there.

A castle is really a fort

with walls all around it.

Lord James's castle

is a very safe place.

Besides the stone walls,

a deep moat runs

around the castle.

A drawbridge can go up

if there is danger.

William and his father stop

at the gatehouse.

The guard raises a heavy gate

called a portcullis.

(You say it like this: port-CULL-iss.)

Now they can go inside.

The lord's family, his knights,
and his servants live in the castle.
This part of the castle is the keep.
The keep is a big tower.
The kitchen, dining hall, chapel,
and bedrooms are here.

William says good-bye to his father.

He is sad.

But there are many other pages.

He will have lots of friends.

William soon finds out

that being a page is hard work!

Pages take care of the hunting dogs.

They run errands.

They bring food to the table.

Everyone drinks ale—including children.

Most people don't have plates.

They use stale slices of bread.

And nobody uses forks—

but not because they have bad manners.

There aren't any forks in England.
They do not come into use
for another 200 years!
Instead, people eat with spoons,
knives, and their fingers.

Many knights live in the castle.

Pages love to hear the knights' stories.

A knight must be loyal to his lord
and to the church.

He must be brave and fair—
even to his enemies.

He must help anyone in trouble.

The pages are very young.

But right away they learn

how to do mock fighting in a joust.

They use small swords and lances.

Here William is tilting at the quintain.

(You say it like this: KWIN-tayn.)

He must knock over

a heavy dummy with his lance.

But William forgets the most

important part—to duck.

The quintain swings around.

William is knocked right off his horse!

Here are some of the other weapons that a knight uses:

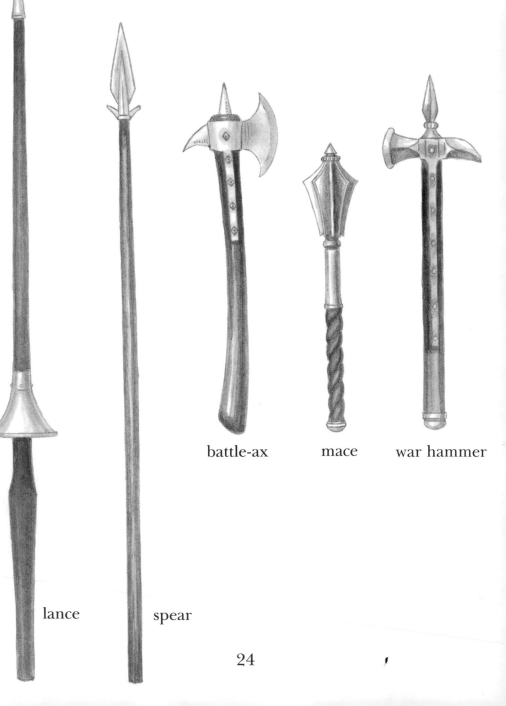

lance   spear   battle-ax   mace   war hammer

dagger

sword

Knights don't use slingshots.

Only peasants use them.

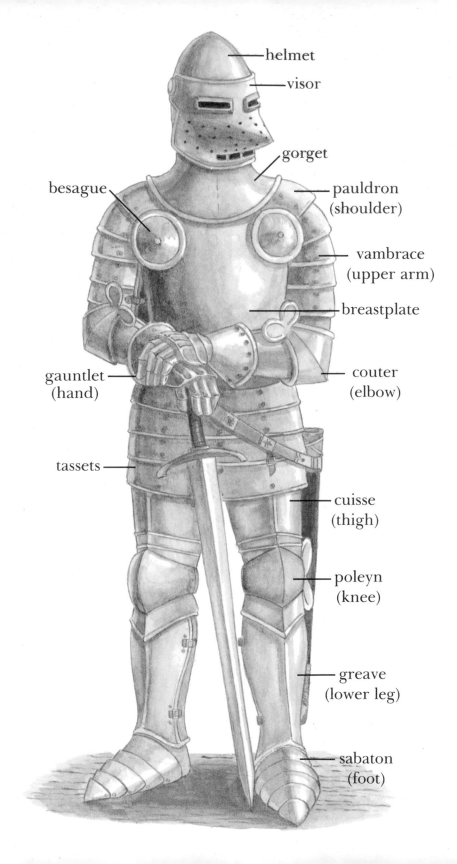

helmet

visor

gorget

besague

pauldron
(shoulder)

vambrace
(upper arm)

breastplate

gauntlet
(hand)

couter
(elbow)

tassets

cuisse
(thigh)

poleyn
(knee)

greave
(lower leg)

sabaton
(foot)

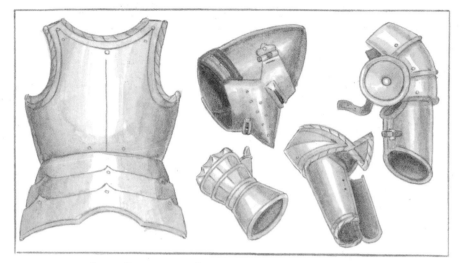

Pages also learn about armor.

A suit of armor may have sixty pieces,

and it weighs about sixty pounds.

Even so, it does not feel heavy to wear.

It just feels very hot inside.

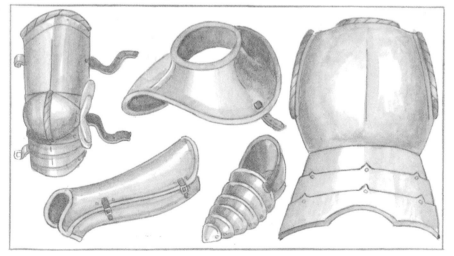

One of the most important pieces

is the shield.

Knights use their shields

to protect themselves.

Each knight puts a special design

on his shield.

It is called his coat of arms.

That way, knights can be told apart

even in their armor.

After William's father dies,

his coat of arms will be passed to William.

Much of William's time is spent
training for war and learning to be
a polite gentleman.

Still, there is time for fun.

Everyone enjoys games such as
chess, checkers, and backgammon.

William likes hoodman's blind
best of all.

It is a lot like blindman's bluff.

Pages also learn to sing and
dance and play the lute.

Sometimes the pages go hunting
with the lords and ladies.
Everyone hopes to catch a stag—
that's a male deer.
Catching a boar or a wolf or a bear
is good too.
But nobody cares about catching
a rabbit—that's for peasants.

Lord James raises falcons

for hunting small birds.

He sets out on horseback.

A hooded falcon sits on his wrist.

When Lord James spots a bird,

he removes the hood.

The falcon goes after the bird.

Then Lord James blows a whistle.

The falcon returns to him,

and a dog brings back the dead bird.

Many times, troubadours

(you say it like this: TROO-ba-doors)

come to the castle.

They sing songs.

They also tell stories about love

and brave knights of old.

Here is one of William's favorites:

Saint George and the Dragon

Saint George was a young knight

who set out to find his fortune.

Soon he came to a town.

A fire-breathing dragon lived nearby.

The villagers had to give

their children to the dragon.

Or else he would set the town on fire.

At last it was the king's turn.

His daughter was named Sabra.

And she was very brave.

She saw Saint George coming

to save her.

She told him to save himself instead.

Did Saint George leave her? No!

He killed the dragon with his sword.

William hopes to be as brave
as Saint George someday.

Today is a special day.

There is going to be a tournament.

(You say it like this: TOOR-na-ment.)

A tournament is like a fake battle.

Knights fight each other.

But blunt weapons are usually used—

not sharp ones.

Everyone comes to watch.

They cheer for their favorite knight.

And each knight ties a scarf

from his favorite lady on his lance.

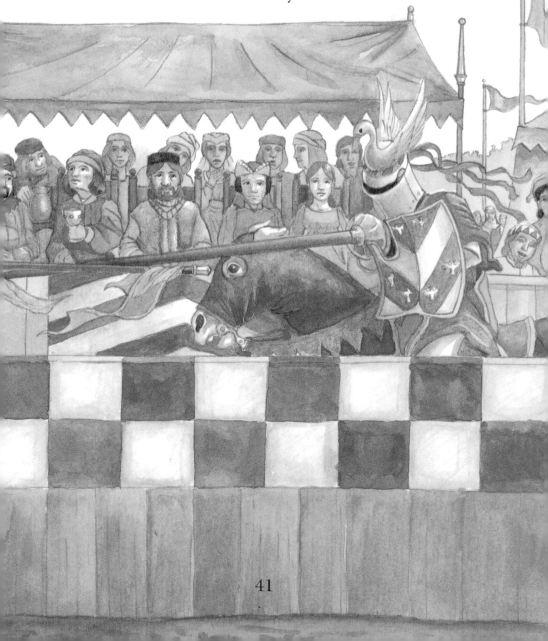

After the tournament, there is a big feast.

Jugglers and actors perform.

There is lots of wine and fancy food.

A cooked swan is served

with all its feathers put back on.

There is a pastry castle with meats,

eggs, and nuts inside it.

Then William sees a most amazing sight.

A large pie is brought in.

A servant slices into it—

and live birds fly out!

The feast lasts far into the night,

long after William and the other

pages have gone to sleep.

William dreams of the day

when he will turn fifteen.

Then he will become a squire.

A squire's job is to serve his knight.

At meals, he carves the knight's meat.

He helps him with his armor.

He takes care of his horse.

He fights by his side in battle.

Squires wear silver spurs.

Only knights wear golden spurs.

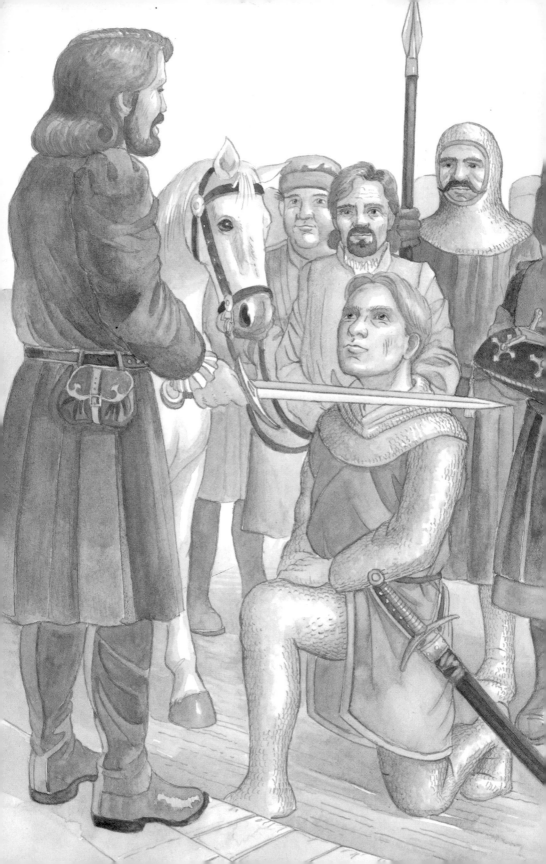

Not all squires become knights.

Usually it is a reward

for a brave deed in battle.

A squire must take the vows

of knighthood.

He kneels before the lord.

The lord touches his shoulders

with a sword.

He presents him with golden spurs.

Now he is a knight!

William looks forward

to the day he may hear the words:

"I dub thee knight!"

Then he will be Sir William.